The Glow: How to Lead with Light and Live with Purpose
by Kimly Hoang-Nakata, M.Ed.

© 2025 Kimly Hoang -Nakata.
All rights reserved.
No part of this book may be reproduced, stored in a retrieval system, or transmitted in any form or by any means —electronic, mechanical, photocopying, recording, or otherwise —without the prior written permission of the author.

For every woman who's ever forgotten her light — may you find it again and let it shine brighter than before.

Contents

Introduction 1
Chapter 1: Defining My Glow Again 3
Chapter 2: Healing the Inner Critic 7
Chapter 3: Emotional Mastery 11
Chapter 4: Strengthening My Structure 15
Chapter 5: Career Strategy & Visibility 19
Chapter 6: Balance Home & Heart 23
Chapter 7: Financial Freedom & Flow 26
Chapter 8: Connection, Community & Contribution 30
Chapter 9: Lead with Glow 34
Chapter 10: Reflect, Recalibrate, and Rise 38

Introduction

Reclaiming My Glow
There was a time when I felt invisible — not because the world couldn't see me, but because I couldn't see myself.
I was a teacher, a graduate student, and a new mother all at once — juggling lesson plans, research papers, and sleepless nights with a baby who needed me more than I knew how to give. On the outside, I seemed capable, strong, and endlessly giving. But inside, I was running on empty. The exhaustion settled deep in my bones , the guilt followed me into every quiet moment, and somewhere between the late -night studying and the early morning feedings, I lost sight of the woman I used to be. I knew about resilience — I had studied psychology and neuroscience. I understood the mechanisms of burnout, emotional regulation, and stress. Yet none of my degrees could prepare me for the quiet ache of feeling disconnected from my own joy.

That ache became my turning point.
One night, sitting in the soft glow of a nightlight, I watched my baby breathe. Her tiny chest rising and falling reminded me that life itself is rhythm — inhale, exhale, rise, fall. I realized I had been holding my breath for years. In that moment, something inside me whispered, "It's time to find your glow again."
My "glow" became more than just a feeling — it became a philosophy, a practice, a way of living. It wasn't about perfection or having it all figured out. It was about reconnecting to who I truly was: a woman of light, purpose, and limitless capacity to grow.
Over the years, as I remarried and became a mother of three, I continued to rediscover that glow — not by eliminating the chaos of life, but by learning how to align my mind, body, and soul within it. Through every season — exhaustion, renewal, heartbreak, and joy — I learned that grace and strength can coexist.

This handbook was born from that journey. It's not just my story — it's a mirror for yours.

If you've ever felt unseen, unheard, or unworthy, this is your invitation to pause, reflect, and remember: your light was never lost. It may have flickered, dimmed, or been buried under the weight of responsibility, but it's still there — waiting to be rekindled.

Through the pages ahead, I'll guide you through the same steps that helped me reclaim my own glow — grounded in the science of well-being, the art of leadership, and the grace of self-compassion. Together, we'll explore how to nurture your mind, strengthen your body, and realign your soul so you can lead — not from burnout, but from brilliance.

You don't have to wait until life is calm to begin shining again. You simply have to choose to begin.

So take a deep breath, open your heart, and let's start this journey — back to the brightest, most authentic version of you.

The glow you seek is already within you — waiting to be remembered.

— **Kimly Hoang-Nakata**

Chapter 1: Defining My Glow Again

A story of exhaustion, rediscovery, and alignment.
I remember the nights when the world went quiet, except for the hum of my thoughts and the soft breaths of my baby sleeping beside me. The clock would flash 2:17 a.m., and I'd still be awake — not because my baby needed me, but because my mind wouldn't stop spinning.
I had assignments due for graduate school, lesson plans to finish for my students, bills waiting on the counter, and a mountain of self-doubt pressing against my chest.

By day, I taught full time — smiling, listening, showing up for my students as if I had it all together. By night, I became a one-woman village: cooking, cleaning, studying, and mothering. Somewhere in between, I forgot how to breathe.
There were moments I'd glance in the mirror and barely recognize the woman looking back. Her eyes were dull, her posture tense, her spark — gone. I wasn't depressed; I was disconnected. I had become a machine of responsibility, fueled by guilt and caffeine.
And yet, deep down, I knew I was capable of more than just survival.

The Breaking Point
One night, while feeding my daughter, I found myself whispering: "I don't even know who I am anymore."

The tears came quietly at first — then all at once. It wasn't sadness alone; it was grief for the woman I used to be — curious, joyful, spontaneous. I realized I had poured everything I had into everyone else and left nothing for myself.

In that stillness, holding my baby, I had a thought that changed everything:
If I want to teach my child to shine, I have to remember how to shine myself.
That night became the seed of what I now call my Glow.

Rediscovering the Glow

At first, I didn't even know what "glow" meant. To me, it wasn't about beauty or confidence — it was about aliveness. I wanted to feel connected again — to my body, my mind, my purpose.
So I began with one simple question:
"What makes me feel light?"

Some days, it was a walk at sunrise. Other days, a five-minute meditation while my daughter napped. Some days, it was giving myself permission not to be perfect — to leave the laundry, to breathe, to rest.
I used my background in psychology and neuroscience not as a professional framework, but as a lifeline. **I began to understand that my exhaustion wasn't weakness — it was my nervous system in overdrive.**
My guilt wasn't motherhood — it was a trauma response to chronic overextension.
Through self-awareness and compassion, I started reprogramming the way I spoke to myself.
Instead of:
"You're not doing enough."
I whispered:
"You're doing your best."

Every small act of grace became a neural spark — rewiring the belief that I had to earn rest, love, or worthiness.

New Chapters, New Layers

Years later, I remarried and welcomed two more beautiful children into my life.
I thought balance would come naturally once I had a partner — but life, of course, had its own lessons.
Motherhood, marriage, and career became a new juggling act. The guilt didn't vanish — it evolved. Now it whispered:

"You should be more present."
"You should be more patient."
"You should be more successful."

This time, though, I had tools.

I had learned that glow doesn't mean perfection or peace without chaos — it means keeping your light lit even in the storm.

So I created boundaries. I learned to say no — not from selfishness, but from self-respect.
I built rituals: morning gratitude, evening reflection, weekly family connection nights.
I practiced self-forgiveness when things weren't perfect — **because glow doesn't live in guilt; it lives in grace.**
Slowly, my energy began to shift. My children noticed it too. One night my daughter said,
"Mommy, you smile more now."

That was when I realized: this journey wasn't just for me — it was for them too.

The Glow Philosophy
My Glow Philosophy was born from this lived truth:
When your mind, body, and soul align, you radiate strength, peace, and purpose.

It's not about doing more — it's about being more connected to what matters most.
Glow happens when:
- Your mind is calm enough to listen
- Your body is cared for and rested

- Your soul feels purpose and joy

And from that alignment, success follows naturally — not as a race, but as a rhythm.

Reflection Prompts:
Take a few moments with your journal and reflect:
1. When was the last time you felt truly "alive"? What were you doing?
2. What are you giving too much of yourself to right now — and what are you neglecting?

3. What lies do you tell yourself about rest, worth, or success?
4. What small act of grace can you give yourself this week?

Glow Practice
Tonight, before bed, place your hand over your heart and whisper: "I am allowed to rest. I am allowed to shine. My glow is mine to protect."

Take one slow, deep breath — in for four counts, out for six — and imagine your inner light gently expanding.
That's the first step toward reclaiming your Glow.

Chapter 2: Healing the Inner Critic

Learning to speak to myself with the same kindness I gave to everyone else.
There was a time when I could stand in front of a classroom full of students and inspire them to believe in their potential — yet come home and whisper to myself that I wasn't good enough.
I could remind a child, "You're doing great, just keep trying," but if I missed a deadline, forgot a permission slip, or showed up five minutes late to daycare pickup, my inner voice would sting like a whip:
"You're failing."
"You should be better by now."
"You're never going to catch up."

I didn't realize it then, but I was living with a silent bully in my own mind — the voice of my inner critic.

The Voice That Never Slept
It followed me everywhere.
When my first child was born and I was juggling bottles, textbooks, and lesson plans, it whispered,
"Other moms seem to handle this better."

When I remarried and became a mother of three, it grew louder:
"You're not giving enough attention to each child."
"Your students deserve more energy."
"You're falling behind in everything."

And when I finally had a moment to rest, it changed its tone:
"You don't deserve to rest."

That was the cruelest lie of all — that love, rest, and peace were things I had to earn.

The Moment of Realization
One afternoon, I was sitting in my car outside of work, engine running, hands gripping the steering wheel. My chest felt tight, like I couldn't catch my breath.
I had just dropped my kids off and was about to rush into another packed day — but something inside me said, Stop.
I turned off the ignition and sat in silence.
Then a single thought came, so clear it almost felt like a whisper from somewhere higher:
"You would never speak to your children the way you speak to yourself."

That sentence broke me open.
I realized I had spent years being my own harshest teacher, my most relentless critic. And somewhere along the way, I had forgotten how to be my own friend.

Understanding the Inner Critic
From my background in psychology and neuroscience, I knew that the inner critic isn't born cruel — it's formed from fear.
It's the brain's way of protecting us from rejection, shame, and failure.
It's the leftover voice of perfectionism, childhood conditioning, cultural expectations, and unhealed wounds.
My critic believed it was helping me — that if it pushed hard enough, I would finally feel "enough."
But what it really did was keep me in a constant state of tension, never able to rest in my own worth.
So I began studying my own mind the way I studied human behavior — with curiosity, not judgment.

The Science of Self-Compassion
I learned that when we shame ourselves, the brain releases cortisol — the same stress hormone triggered in survival mode.
But when we practice self-compassion, even in small moments, the body releases oxytocin — the same hormone of safety and connection we feel when we hold a child or receive a hug.

So I decided to start small.
When the voice said,
"You're behind,"
I answered,
"I'm doing my best, and that's enough for today."
When it said,
"You're not a good mom,"
I replied,
"I'm a loving mom. My children know they're loved."

At first it felt awkward — like speaking a new language. But slowly, it began to rewire me. My thoughts softened. My body relaxed. I started to notice joy in small moments again.

Replacing Criticism with Compassion
I created a new rule for myself — one that changed everything:
If I wouldn't say it to my child or my best friend, I don't say it to myself.

That became my mantra.
Instead of focusing on what I lacked, I began celebrating what I had done well — even the smallest victories.
Got everyone dressed and fed? That counts.
Made it through a hard day with patience (mostly)? That counts too.

Took five minutes for deep breathing before bed? That's self-love in action. I realized that progress doesn't come from punishment — it comes from permission.
Permission to rest.
Permission to learn.
Permission to shine at your own pace.

When the Critic Returns
Even now, my inner critic hasn't disappeared completely.
She still visits when I take on too much, when I feel stretched thin, or when old fears resurface.
But now, I recognize her voice instantly. I greet her with grace:

"I see you. You're scared. But we're safe now."

That's the difference between then and now — I no longer silence her with shame; I soothe her with compassion.

And every time I do, my Glow gets brighter.

Reflection Prompts:
Take a quiet moment with your journal and answer:
1. What phrases or thoughts does your inner critic repeat most often?
2. Where do you think those voices originated — a parent, a teacher, society, your own expectations?
3. What does your most compassionate self sound like? Write down her words.
4. How would your day change if you spoke to yourself with the same kindness you give to others?

Glow Practice
Tonight, stand in front of the mirror.
Look into your own eyes — not to check your flaws, but to find the person
who's been trying so hard.
Place your hand on your heart and say aloud:
"I am proud of the woman I'm becoming."
"I forgive myself for expecting perfection."
"I am learning, and that is enough."

Smile softly.
That moment — that breath of self-recognition — is where your healing begins.

Chapter 3: Emotional Mastery

Learning to Lead My Energy, Not Just My Life

I used to think emotional strength meant not crying — that if I just held it together long enough, I'd prove I could handle anything.
So I did what many women do: I smiled through exhaustion, powered through heartache, and told myself to "just keep going."
And on the outside, it looked like I was doing great — a devoted mother, a hardworking teacher, a graduate student managing it all.
But inside, I was drowning in quiet waves of overwhelm.

When the Mind is Loud and the Heart is Tired

There was one afternoon — I remember it vividly — when everything seemed to happen at once.
My oldest had a fever, my middle child spilled juice all over a project I had spent hours preparing, and my baby refused to nap.
My phone buzzed with work messages I hadn't answered yet, and my own body was screaming for rest.
I remember standing in the kitchen, surrounded by chaos, and feeling this wave of heat rise up from my chest to my throat — the kind that makes you want to scream, cry, and collapse all at once.
But I didn't.
I swallowed it down, plastered on a tired smile, and said softly, "It's okay, Mommy's fine."
Except I wasn't.
That night, after the kids were asleep, I sat on the bathroom floor and cried. Not because of the mess, but because I had realized something painful — I was teaching my children how to ignore their emotions by ignoring my own.

The Moment of Awareness

With my background in psychology and neuroscience, I knew that unprocessed emotions don't disappear — they get stored. The body keeps score.
Stress that isn't released becomes tension.
Words unspoken become headaches.

Unfelt sadness becomes irritability.
I had spent years managing life but not leading my energy. I was living in survival mode — my nervous system constantly switched to "fight or flight." That realization changed everything. I decided it was time to stop silencing my emotions and start listening to them.

Listening Instead of Suppressing
I began small. The next time I felt anger rising, instead of snapping or swallowing it, I paused.
I took a deep breath and asked myself:
"What are you really feeling right now?"

Sometimes it was frustration. Sometimes sadness. Sometimes fear that I was failing.
By naming it, I noticed the feeling would lose some of its power — almost like it just wanted to be acknowledged.
That's when I learned a truth that shifted my entire perspective:
Emotions are messengers, not enemies.

They arrive to tell us something:

- Anger says, "A boundary has been crossed."
- Sadness says, "Something needs to be grieved."
- Anxiety says, "You're trying to control what you can't."

When I stopped fighting my feelings and started listening, I began to understand myself again.

The Power of the Pause
One of the most life-changing habits I developed was what I call The Sacred Pause.
Before reacting — to my children, to my partner, to stress — I trained myself to pause for just three seconds.
Breathe in.
Notice the emotion.
Exhale before responding.
It sounds simple, but those three seconds became sacred ground — the space where I chose peace over reaction.

And slowly, something shifted.
My tone softened.
My patience grew.
My children mirrored that calm back to me.
Because the truth is: **our energy teaches louder than our words ever will.**

Emotional Leadership in Motherhood and Work
As a teacher and a mom, I began to see emotional regulation as a form of leadership.
If I could model calm in chaos, my students and my children would learn calm too.
If I could admit mistakes with grace, they'd learn self-compassion.
If I could show emotions in healthy ways, they'd learn that vulnerability isn't weakness — it's wisdom.
Leadership isn't just managing tasks; it's managing presence.
And that's what emotional mastery really is: learning to lead your energy before you lead anything else.

What Neuroscience Teaches Us About Calm
I often explain to my students and other mothers that the brain has two main responses:
- The reactive brain (the amygdala), which triggers fight, flight, or freeze
- The reflective brain (the prefrontal cortex), which helps us think clearly and respond intentionally

The key is learning how to shift from reaction to reflection.
Every time we pause to breathe, journal, or name a feeling, we strengthen the pathways between those two brain regions.
Over time, this rewires how we experience stress — making peace our default state, not panic.

Emotional Freedom Takes Practice
Emotional mastery doesn't mean we stop feeling — it means we stop letting our emotions drive the car.
Some days, I still lose my temper.
Some days, I cry in the car.
But now, instead of seeing those moments as failure, I see them as

feedback.
Because mastery isn't perfection — it's awareness.

When you can name your emotion, breathe through it, and choose your response, you've already reclaimed your power.

Reflection Prompts:
Take a quiet moment for yourself and reflect:
1. What emotions do you tend to suppress or avoid the most — and why?
2. What situations trigger your strongest reactions?
3. How can you build your own "Sacred Pause" habit this week?
4. What emotion needs to be felt and released right now?

Glow Practice: The 3-Minute Reset
Whenever you feel overwhelmed or triggered, try this short practice:
1. Pause – Stop what you're doing and take one deep breath.
2. Name it – Say aloud: "I feel ___."
3. Soothe it – Place your hand over your heart, breathe out longer than you breathe in, and whisper, "I'm safe. I'm okay."
Do this three times. Notice the shift in your body.
That moment of calm — that's you leading your energy. That's you glowing.

Chapter 4: Strengthening My Structure

Rebuilding My Body and Energy from the Inside Out

There was a season in my life when I woke up already exhausted. Not because I hadn't slept — though that, too, was often true — but because my energy was constantly being spent before the day even began.

Before my feet touched the floor, my mind was already racing: lunches to pack, deadlines to meet, emails to answer, classes to teach, dinner to plan. I would look at my reflection, hair in a messy bun, eyes tired but determined, and whisper, "Come on, you can do this."

And I could.

But just because I could didn't mean I was meant to live that way forever.

When My Body Became the Silent Messenger

I didn't realize how disconnected I had become from my body until it started talking to me — in the language of aches, fatigue, and tension. My back hurt constantly. My shoulders carried invisible weight. My chest felt tight even when I wasn't anxious.

I blamed stress, lack of sleep, maybe age. But deep down, I knew it was something deeper — my body wasn't just tired; it was overlooked.

I had spent years taking care of everyone else's needs — my students, my children, my family — but I couldn't remember the last time I'd asked my body what it needed.

The Turning Point

One morning, I was rushing to get the kids out the door, coffee in hand, when my oldest said,

"Mommy, you never sit with us anymore."

It stopped me cold.

She was right. I was always moving — cooking, cleaning, answering messages, checking things off lists — but rarely present.

That night, I lay awake and realized something powerful:

I had been treating my body like a vehicle — something to push harder, fuel occasionally, and ignore until it broke down.

But the body isn't a machine. It's a messenger. It tells us when we're out of alignment — physically, emotionally, and spiritually.
And mine had been whispering for years.

Reconnecting with My Physical Glow
The next morning, I started differently.
I woke up before my children — not to work, but to breathe.
Five slow breaths.
Hands over my heart.
A quiet thank you to my body for carrying me this far.
That single act — gratitude for the body I had been criticizing for years — began to heal something deeper.
I stopped exercising to punish myself and started moving to nourish myself. Sometimes it was yoga with my kids climbing over me, sometimes a walk after dinner, sometimes just dancing in the kitchen while dinner cooked.

I also started drinking water before coffee — it sounds small, but it was symbolic. I was finally choosing hydration before hustle.

The Neuroscience of Energy
From my studies in neuroscience, I understood that energy isn't just physical — it's electrical and emotional.
Our brain, nervous system, and hormones constantly communicate through the body's inner wiring.
When we're chronically stressed, our nervous system stays in a state of fight or flight — cortisol spikes, adrenaline floods, and rest becomes impossible.
But when we take small, mindful actions — deep breathing, stretching, gratitude — the body shifts into rest and repair.
This activates the parasympathetic system, lowering heart rate and allowing the brain to release serotonin and oxytocin — the "peace and connection" chemicals.
That's when our true energy — our glow — begins to return.

Learning to Rest Without Guilt
Rest used to feel like a luxury to me — something I'd "earn" after I finished everything on my list.
But I realized that list was never -ending.
So I made a new rule:
"Rest is not a reward. Rest is my responsibility." I

began taking five -minute pauses throughout the day — no phone, no task, just breathing.
I stretched between meetings. I stepped outside to feel sunlight. I replaced guilt with gratitude.

And slowly, my body began to respond.
The tension eased. The fog lifted. I could feel my energy returning — not the kind fueled by caffeine, but the kind that comes from alignment.

Modeling Health for My Children
As I strengthened my structure, I began to notice how my children mirrored me.
When I rushed, they rushed.
When I paused, they softened.
When I practiced gratitude for my body — instead of criticizing it — they began to thank theirs, too.
It struck me that teaching them healthy habits wasn't just about nutrition or sleep; it was about modeling energy respect.
When they saw me rest without shame, they learned that peace was power, not weakness.
When they saw me move joyfully, they learned that health could be love, not discipline.
That's what true generational wellness looks like — not inherited guilt, but inherited grace.

Reflection Prompts:
Take a few moments to reflect:
1. How does your body try to communicate with you when you're overwhelmed or misaligned?
2. What does "energy" mean to you — and what drains or restores it most?
3. What small physical rituals could you add this week to honor your body's needs?
4. How do your self-care choices influence your family's energy or rhythm?

Glow Practice: The "Body Check-In" Ritual
Each morning, take one minute before you start your day to connect with your body.
- Step 1: Close your eyes and ask, "What does my body need right now?"
- Step 2: Scan from head to toe, noticing areas of tension or fatigue.
- Step 3: Place your hand over that area, breathe deeply, and whisper, "I'm listening."

Then, do one kind thing for your body that day — stretch, hydrate, nap, or simply rest your shoulders.
Your body has carried you through storms and miracles alike. It deserves your love, not your last.

Chapter 5: Career Strategy & Visibility

Learning to Stand Tall and Be Seen with Confidence

There was a time when I thought that hard work spoke for itself — that if I just kept showing up, doing my best, and quietly going the extra mile, someone would notice.
For years, I believed that visibility was vanity, that humility meant silence, and that being a good woman meant being agreeable.
And so, I stayed small — not because I lacked ambition, but because I was afraid of being too much.
Too opinionated.
Too bold.
Too confident.
Too loud.
What I didn't realize then was that I wasn't being humble. I was being hidden.

When My Glow Dimmed Under Self-Doubt
I remember sitting in a meeting one afternoon, surrounded by colleagues I respected. I had worked late the night before preparing ideas for a new program. When the discussion turned toward that very topic, I hesitated — waiting for the right moment to speak.
But before I could, someone else shared an almost identical idea — and the room lit up with praise.
I smiled politely, but my heart sank. It wasn't about the credit; it was about the silence I had chosen.
Driving home that day, I kept replaying the moment in my head — the fear that had held my voice hostage.
"What if I sound unprepared?"
"What if they don't take me seriously?"
"What if I fail publicly?"

But somewhere inside, another voice whispered, softer but stronger:
"What if you're meant to be heard?"

The Realization: My Silence Wasn't Humility — It Was Fear
That was my turning point. I realized I had spent so much of my career hiding behind competence instead of stepping into confidence.
As a teacher, a leader, and a mother, I encouraged others to use their voices — yet mine trembled when I tried to use it for myself.
From my background in psychology and neuroscience, I knew what was happening: my brain had learned to associate visibility with risk.
Our nervous system doesn't distinguish between real and perceived danger — public speaking, advocating for a raise, or disagreeing with authority can trigger the same fear circuits as physical threat.
So my mind did what it was trained to do — protect me. But in doing so, it also kept me small.

The Work of Becoming Seen
Visibility isn't about being loud; it's about being present.
It's about walking into a room and knowing that your value doesn't depend on permission.
I began practicing what I now call "confident calm" — grounded visibility. Before meetings, I would pause, place my hand over my heart, and remind myself:
"You belong here. You've earned this seat. Speak from truth, not fear."

At first, my voice still shook. But each time I spoke up, the shaking lessened.
Each time I stood up for my ideas, the ground beneath me felt steadier.
Soon, something beautiful began to happen:
People started listening — not because I demanded it, but because I believed I had something worth saying.

Redefining Ambition
Motherhood had once made me feel like I had to choose: career or family, ambition or peace.
But as I grew, I realized those weren't opposites — they were allies.
My children became my reason, not my excuse.
I wanted them to see what it looked like when a woman led with authenticity — when she balanced empathy with excellence, grace with grit.

Success stopped being about climbing ladders and started being about expanding influence.
I wanted to lead in a way that lifted others, not just myself.

That's when my glow began to radiate differently — not as a spotlight on me, but as a light that illuminated others too.

What Science Says About Confidence
Neuroscience shows that confidence isn't a fixed trait — it's a skill built through repetition and emotional safety.
Every time we take small courageous actions — sharing an idea, setting a boundary, advocating for ourselves — our brain's confidence pathways strengthen.
Dopamine (the motivation chemical) rewards the action, making it easier next time.
The secret isn't waiting to feel confident before acting.
It's acting while afraid — and letting confidence catch up.

The Rise of My Professional Glow
As I began showing up more boldly, new opportunities began to appear.
People noticed my perspective. My students and colleagues began coming to me for advice.
And something miraculous happened — not because I became someone new, but because I finally allowed the real me to be seen.
The glow I had been searching for wasn't out there in recognition or titles; it was in the courage to be visible and authentic at the same time.

Reflection Prompts:
Pause here and take a moment to reflect:
1. In what areas of your career or life do you hold back your voice — and why?
2. What fears come up when you imagine being fully seen?
3. What is one small, bold action you can take this week to step into visibility?
4. How can you celebrate your wins without guilt or apology?

Glow Practice: The Power Pose of Presence

Before an important meeting, conversation, or moment where you want to feel grounded and confident, try this:

1. Stand tall. Feet shoulder-width apart, shoulders back, chin lifted.
2. Breathe in deeply. Imagine light filling your body with calm strength.
3. Say quietly to yourself: "I am enough. I belong in every room I enter."
4. Smile gently. Not for approval — but as a declaration of self-assurance.

Confidence isn't about being fearless. It's about showing up — even when your heart races — and realizing you can trust yourself to shine.

Chapter 6: Balance Home & Heart

Redefining What "Having It All" Really Means
There was a time when "balance" felt like a cruel joke.
I used to imagine it as this serene, Pinterest-perfect picture — color-coded calendars, organic meals, happy kids, folded laundry, lesson plans done early, all while maintaining a calm smile.
But my real life? It was juggling dinner while answering emails, helping one child with homework while calming a crying baby, and trying to remember if I'd actually eaten lunch that day.
There were nights I'd collapse into bed, not because the day was done, but because I was.
And yet, I'd still whisper to myself, "Tomorrow, I'll do better."
That phrase became a quiet trap — because no matter how hard I tried, "better" always moved just out of reach.

The Breaking Point of "Doing It All"
One evening, after another long day of teaching and mothering, I found myself in tears over something small — a spilled bowl of cereal.
It wasn't about the cereal, of course. It was about everything it represented — the constant motion, the invisible labor, the impossible standards.
I felt guilty for being tired, guilty for needing space, guilty for wanting more balance when I already had so much to be grateful for.
That night, as I sat in the dark living room with the hum of the dishwasher in the background, I whispered:
"I can't keep living like this."

And my heart answered, softly:
"Then don't."

That was the beginning of my home and heart transformation — **the realization that balance isn't something you find; it's something you create.**

The Myth of "Having It All"
As women, we're told we can have it all — career, family, success, health, joy — but no one tells us the truth:
You can have it all, just not all at once and not all by yourself.
Balance doesn't mean splitting your time equally — it means aligning your energy intentionally.
I started asking myself three questions every morning:
1. What truly needs my attention today?
2. What can wait?
3. What can I release — without guilt?

Those questions became my compass.
I learned that "no" is not rejection; it's redirection.
That rest isn't laziness; it's leadership.
That peace is not something you find in stillness — it's something you protect in motion.

Building Systems of Support
When I remarried and became a mother of three, I made a promise to myself: I would not carry it all alone.
So I began building what I call my Support Structure — small systems that held my home and heart steady.
• Shared Responsibility: My partner and I divided tasks based on strength, not stereotype.
• Family Rhythms: We created weekly rituals — Sunday prep, gratitude dinners, tech-free evenings.
• Simplification: I let go of perfection. Frozen pizza nights, paper plates, and messy kitchens were no longer signs of failure — they were signs of humanity.
And most importantly, I started asking for help without shame. Because asking for help doesn't make you weak — it invites connection.

The Science of Balance
From a neuroscience perspective, chronic multitasking keeps the brain's stress circuits activated.
Each "switch" between tasks releases small bursts of cortisol, which over time leads to exhaustion, irritability, and decreased focus.
True balance isn't found in doing more efficiently — it's found in doing

less intentionally.

By focusing on one thing at a time — a mindful conversation, a meal with your kids, a quiet breath — you actually regulate your nervous system, improve emotional stability, and boost long-term energy.
In other words, slowing down saves your brain.

The New Definition of "All"
Today, when I say I have it all, it means something very different than it used to.
It doesn't mean everything is perfect. It means my life finally feels mine. I have joy and exhaustion, laughter and mess, ambition and grace — and I've stopped seeing them as contradictions.
Balance is not the absence of chaos — it's the presence of peace within it. And that, I've learned, is where my glow truly lives — not in getting it all done, but in being fully present for what matters most.

Reflection Prompts:
Pause here, and take a few deep breaths before writing:
1. What expectations of "having it all" are you ready to release?
2. What does balance really look and feel like for you — in this season of life?
3. What small shift could bring more peace into your daily rhythm?
4. Who can you ask for help — and what's stopping you from asking?

Glow Practice:
The Evening Reset Ritual Each evening, take five quiet minutes to reset your energy before bed.
1. Sit or lie down. Close your eyes and breathe deeply.
2. Ask yourself: o What drained me today? What filled me today?
3. Whisper: "I release what's heavy. I keep what's light."
4. Imagine the stress melting away — your mind softening, your heart opening.

This small ritual teaches your body and brain to separate the day's noise from your true peace.
And when you wake up the next morning, you'll notice — your heart feels lighter, and your glow feels closer.

Chapter 7: Financial Freedom & Flow

Building Stability with Soul
Money was always one of those topics that made me feel both driven and uneasy.
As a single mother working full-time and going to graduate school, money was survival. It wasn't about luxury — it was about keeping the lights on, paying for childcare, and praying my car wouldn't break down before the next paycheck.
I learned early how to stretch a dollar and smile through the stress. But deep down, I carried a quiet, constant fear: What if it all falls apart?
That fear followed me, even after my life began to stabilize. I had a family, a career, a home — and yet the old anxiety lingered, whispering that it could all disappear.

It took years for me to understand that financial freedom starts long before you ever have "enough."
It begins with healing your relationship with money.

The Emotional Weight of Money
Money, I discovered, is never just about numbers.
It's about safety. It's about self-worth. It's about the stories we grew up believing.
I grew up hearing phrases like,
"You have to work twice as hard to make it."
"Money doesn't grow on trees."
"Be grateful for what you have."

They were meant to teach humility and discipline — and they did. But they also planted seeds of guilt and limitation.
So even when I worked hard and earned more, I subconsciously sabotaged my peace. I felt guilty for wanting stability. I over gave, overspent on others, and undervalued my own needs.
It wasn't greed I feared — it was the feeling of being undeserving.

The Turning Point
One night, after the kids were asleep, I sat at the kitchen table with a stack of bills and my laptop open to my bank account.
The numbers weren't terrible — but I felt terrible.
I realized I wasn't stressed because of what I had or didn't have. I was stressed because of what money represented — pressure, fear, responsibility.
And then it hit me:

"I've been treating money the same way I used to treat myself — with distrust and guilt."

That realization stopped me cold.
I had done so much inner work to heal my mind and body — but not my money story.
So I decided to start seeing money the way I saw energy: something that flows when respected, but stagnates when resisted.

Reframing Money Through the Lens of Energy
From my background in psychology and neuroscience, I knew that beliefs shape behavior, and behavior shapes outcomes.
When you associate money with fear or scarcity, your brain activates its survival circuits — the same ones triggered by physical danger. Cortisol rises, decision -making narrows, and long -term planning becomes difficult. But when you shift to a mindset of trust and flow, the brain releases dopamine and serotonin — chemicals that enhance clarity, creativity, and optimism.
In simple terms:
Fear blocks flow.
Gratitude creates it.
So I started small. Every time I paid a bill, I whispered,
"Thank you for the resources that made this possible."
When I received a paycheck, I paused to feel genuine appreciation — not just for the amount, but for the exchange of my purpose for prosperity. Slowly, money stopped being a source of tension and started becoming a teacher.

Practical Steps Toward Freedom
As my mindset shifted, I began building structure around my finances — simple, sustainable habits that supported stability:
1. Automation: I set up automatic savings and bill payments. Every dollar had a destination — and that clarity brought peace.
2. Awareness: I reviewed my spending weekly, not to judge, but to understand what aligned with my values.
3. Boundaries: I learned to say no — not only to others, but to my own impulsive "I deserve this" moments that came from emotional fatigue.
4. Education: I read, listened, learned. Financial literacy became my new form of empowerment. It wasn't about chasing wealth — it was about creating a system where I could breathe again.

Money as a Mirror
One afternoon, while teaching a lesson on growth mindset to my students, I heard myself say,
"We can't grow if we're afraid to make mistakes."
And I realized — the same was true for money.
For years, I had avoided investing, negotiating, and expanding because I was afraid to make a "wrong" move. But mistakes are part of mastery.
The first time I asked for a raise, my voice shook. But I reminded myself — this isn't just about money; it's about modeling self-worth.
And when that raise came through, I didn't just celebrate the amount — I celebrated the shift: from scarcity to self-respect.

Teaching My Children Financial Wholeness
As my relationship with money healed, I began teaching my children something different — that money is not a measure of worth, but a tool for freedom and generosity.
We talk openly about saving, giving, and spending with intention. They see me donate to causes I care about, invest in learning, and also say no when something doesn't align.
Because true abundance isn't having more — it's feeling at peace with what you have and confident in your ability to create more when needed. That's financial glow.

Reflection Prompts:
Take a few quiet minutes to journal or think through these questions:
1. What stories did you grow up believing about money?
2. How do those stories still show up in your decisions today?
3. What does "financial freedom" mean to you — emotionally, not just materially?
4. What one habit could you start this week to bring more peace and structure to your finances?

Glow Practice: The Gratitude Transaction
Each time you pay a bill, buy a meal, or receive income, pause for a single breath and say:
"Thank you for the flow of energy in and out of my life."

Visualize that exchange as light — money leaving your hands to support others and returning to you in new forms of opportunity, peace, and purpose.

When you honor money with mindfulness, it begins to honor you with ease. And that's how financial glow begins — not with wealth alone, but with the wisdom to flow.

Chapter 8: Connection, Community & Contribution

The Power of Women Rising Together
There's a quote I once read that said,
"You can't pour from an empty cup, but once it's full — let it overflow."

For most of my life, I thought I had to choose between giving to others and taking care of myself. I'd pour and pour — into my students, my children, my relationships — until there was nothing left.
When I finally began to heal, I learned that true contribution doesn't come from depletion. It comes from overflow.
And that overflow — that radiant energy of purpose and giving — doesn't happen in isolation.
It happens in connection.

The Loneliness Beneath the Strength
As a working mother, I learned how to appear strong even when I was unraveling.

I smiled through exhaustion. I said "I'm fine" when I wasn't.
But the truth was, there were nights I'd feel painfully alone — not because I lacked people around me, but because I felt unseen.
It's a silent struggle many women carry: we're surrounded, but isolated.
We're needed, but not always nourished.

One day, after a particularly rough week, I sat in my car outside the school parking lot — the same spot where so many of my realizations had come — and thought, I need other women who get it.
Not to fix me. Not to judge me. Just to remind me I'm not alone in this journey.
That realization changed the course of my life and career.

Finding My Circle
It started small.
A few of us — working mothers, educators, women navigating our own versions of chaos — began meeting after work once a month.
No agenda. No expectations. Just honesty.
We called it our "Glow Circle."
We talked about everything — motherhood, marriage, dreams, burnout, boundaries, finances, faith.
Sometimes we cried. Sometimes we laughed until our faces hurt. And every time we left those meetings, we felt lighter. Stronger. Seen. That's when I realized:
"Healing multiplies in community."
We weren't fixing each other — we were reflecting light back at each other.

The Science of Connection
In neuroscience, we call it co-regulation — the process by which human nervous systems calm and stabilize each other through presence, empathy, and attunement.
When you share openly with someone who listens with compassion, your body releases oxytocin — the hormone of bonding and trust. Your heart rate steadies. Your brain quiets. Your energy returns.

It's not just emotional — it's biological.
We are wired to heal in connection.
That's why isolation feels heavy, and why genuine relationships feel like a breath of fresh air.
Connection doesn't just feel good — it's medicine for the mind and body.

Giving as a Form of Growth
As I began to feel stronger, I noticed something shift: the more I gave from a full heart, the more my own glow expanded.
Contribution, I realized, wasn't about grand gestures — it was about presence.
It was listening to a colleague who needed support.
Encouraging a student who doubted herself.

Leaving a kind note for another mother who looked tired at pickup.
When I stopped trying to give perfectly and started giving authentically, giving became energizing — not draining.
And that energy rippled outward.
People began telling me, "You have this calm light about you."
I smiled, knowing it wasn't about perfection. It was about connection.

Redefining Support Among Women
For generations, women have been conditioned to compete — to compare, to measure, to hide their struggles.
But the moment we stop seeing each other as rivals and start seeing each other as reflections, everything changes.
When one woman rises, she lights the path for others.

So I began intentionally surrounding myself with women who were both compassionate and courageous — women who clapped for me when I won, and held space when I didn't.
And I made it my mission to do the same for them.
Because the truth is, glow shared is glow multiplied.

Teaching Connection to My Children
One evening, my daughter asked,
"Mommy, why do you always tell your friends you're proud of them?"

I smiled and said,
"Because when we celebrate others, we remind ourselves that joy isn't scarce."

That's what I want her — and all my children — to know: **that connection is abundance.**
There's no limit to love, encouragement, or light.
And when we live from that truth, life stops feeling like a competition and starts feeling like a symphony.

Reflection Prompts:
Pause here and reflect on these:
1. Who in your life makes you feel seen, supported, and safe?
2. Who drains your energy — and what boundaries need to be set?
3. How can you contribute to someone else's glow this week?
4. What kind of community would help you grow into your next season of life?

Glow Practice: The Ripple of Light
Tonight, think of one woman — a friend, coworker, relative — who's been on your mind.
Send her a simple message:
"Thinking of you. I see how hard you're trying. You inspire me."
No agenda. No need for a reply.
Just one ripple of kindness — a reminder that connection begins with one small act of recognition.
That's how we build circles of light that can illuminate the world.

Chapter 9: Lead with Glow

The Art of Confident, Compassionate Leadership
For years, I believed leadership was about titles, authority, or expertise.
I thought to lead meant to have all the answers, to project confidence, to never show cracks.
But when life broke me open — through motherhood, burnout, and renewal — I learned that true leadership doesn't come from control.
It comes from connection.
The Moment I Realized I Was Leading All Along
It wasn't in a meeting or a classroom that I first realized what real leadership meant — it was in my living room.
One morning, I was rushing through my usual routine: packing lunches, searching for shoes, mentally running through my to-do list. My daughter tugged my sleeve and said,
"Mommy, you're talking, but you're not looking at me."

That stopped me.

I knelt down, met her eyes, and listened.
She smiled.
And in that moment, I realized something profound — leadership begins with presence.
It's not about commanding others. It's about seeing them.
It's about being so rooted in who you are that others feel safe to be who they are, too.
That realization would forever change how I led in every area of my life — at home, in my classroom, and beyond.

From Control to Connection
When I first started teaching, I thought being respected meant being firm — maybe even strict.
I confused authority with rigidity.
But over time, I learned that authority built on fear fades quickly, while authority built on empathy lasts a lifetime.
I began to shift my focus from control to connection.
Instead of asking, "How do I get them to listen?" I asked, "How do I help them feel heard?" That change — simple but profound — transformed

not just my classroom, but my life.
My students began to trust me more. My children opened up more.
Even my colleagues started to share ideas more freely.
Because when people feel safe, they shine.
And that, I realized, is leadership: helping others rediscover their own glow.

The Neuroscience of Leadership Energy
Leadership isn't just emotional — it's physiological.
When we lead with calm confidence, we activate mirror neurons in others — specialized brain cells that reflect the emotions and energy of those around us.
That's why one grounded person can change the mood of an entire room. Our nervous systems are constantly syncing.
When we bring peace, others feel it. When we bring chaos, others absorb it.
So every morning, before walking into my classroom or a meeting, I'd pause and take one deep, intentional breath.
"I choose to lead with calm."

That single breath wasn't just for me — it was a signal to everyone around me that they were safe, seen, and supported.

Leadership as a Mirror of Motherhood
Motherhood has been my greatest leadership training ground.
It taught me patience, adaptability, and humility — and it showed me the power of leading with love instead of perfection.
There were times I lost my temper, apologized, and tried again. Times I listened instead of lectured.
Times I let my children teach me what empathy really looks like.
Those moments taught me more about leadership than any course ever could.
Because leadership isn't about getting it right every time — it's about modeling what it looks like to grow, fail, reflect, and rise.

And in that sense, motherhood and leadership are one and the same: both are sacred acts of shaping hearts, including our own.

Standing in Your Light. Lead Without Hesitation.

As women, we're often conditioned to shrink our brilliance — to lead quietly, to avoid being "too much."
But authentic leadership begins with being seen.

It means standing in your truth and letting your presence speak — not with arrogance, but with grounded grace.
Now, whenever I doubt myself, I remind myself of this truth:
"I am not leading for recognition. I am leading from alignment."
And alignment — between who I am and what I give — is where my glow shines brightest.

How to Lead with Glow
Leadership with glow isn't a style — it's a state of being. Here are the principles I now live by:
1. Lead Yourself First.
You can't lead others from chaos. Check in with your energy before you show up.
2. Be Transparent, Not Perfect.
Vulnerability builds trust. Admit when you don't know. People respect honesty over perfection.
3. Listen Deeply.
Real listening isn't waiting to reply — it's holding space for another's truth.
4. Empower, Don't Control.
Leadership isn't about being the loudest voice. It's about helping others find theirs.
5. Reflect and Renew.
Leadership is emotional labor. Protect your peace, refill your energy, and rest without guilt.
6. Serve with Purpose.
Every interaction is a chance to uplift. Your presence is your platform

Reflection Prompts:
Take a moment to sit quietly and write:
1. How do you currently lead — at home, at work, or in your relationships?
2. What kind of energy do you bring into the spaces you enter?
3. Who are the people that make you feel safe to shine — and how can you do the same for others?
4. What kind of leader do you want to be remembered as?

Glow Practice: The Leadership Grounding Ritual
Before any important conversation, meeting, or moment of influence, pause for this 2-minute ritual:
1. Stand tall. Feel your feet grounded, your spine aligned.
2. Place your hand over your heart.
3. Breathe deeply and silently repeat: "I am calm. I am confident. I am connected."
4. Visualize your energy as a soft, steady light radiating outward — touching everyone you meet with empathy, respect, and strength.
That light — that inner calm — is what people will remember long after your words.
That's your leadership glow.

Chapter 10: Reflect, Recalibrate, and Rise

The Continuous Journey of Growth and Grace
There was a time when I believed healing and success had an endpoint — that one day I'd finally arrive: calm, confident, balanced, and unshakably whole.
But what I've learned, through years of mothering, teaching, and learning, is that life doesn't have finish lines — it has cycles.
There are seasons when you rise, seasons when you rest, and seasons when you're simply being rebuilt in silence.

The glow, I discovered, isn't about reaching perfection — it's about remembering your light again and again, no matter how many times the world dims it.

The Year Everything Changed — Again
I remember the year I thought I had it all figured out.
The house was in order, work was flowing, the kids were thriving — for the first time, I felt balanced.
And then, life shifted.
A new challenge arose at work. One of my children began struggling emotionally. I felt the old familiar tightness in my chest, the anxiety whispering, "Here we go again."
For a moment, I panicked — thinking I was "slipping backward." But this time, instead of spiraling, I paused.
I remembered what I had learned: that growth doesn't erase struggle — it gives you the tools to move through it differently.
So I breathed.
I reflected.
And I whispered, "Okay. Let's recalibrate."

That one word — recalibrate — became my anchor.

Reflection: The Power of Honest Looking Back
Reflection isn't about judgment; it's about understanding.
In psychology, reflection allows the brain to integrate experiences — to connect emotion with meaning. It helps transform chaos into clarity.

Every month, I began a ritual: sitting with a journal and asking three questions:
1. What am I proud of?
2. What did I learn?
3. What do I need to release?
Some months, the answers came easily. Other months, they came through tears.
But every time, I left that reflection with a little more grace for myself.
Reflection reminds us that even our hardest moments have taught us something sacred.

Recalibration: The Art of Gentle Adjustment
In physics, recalibration means fine-tuning something to improve accuracy.
In life, it means doing the same — adjusting habits, boundaries, and perspectives to realign with who you're becoming.
I started treating my life like a living experiment, not a performance.
If a schedule wasn't working — I changed it.
If a relationship felt draining — I set new boundaries.
If my body needed rest — I gave it, without guilt.
That's the beauty of recalibration: you don't start over; you realign.
Each adjustment brought me closer to peace — not because life was perfect, but because I was learning to move with it instead of against it.

Rising Again, Differently
There's something powerful about falling and rising — but even more powerful about rising differently.
The woman I am today doesn't measure success by how much I do, but by how aligned I feel.
I've stopped chasing approval and started protecting my peace.
I no longer confuse stillness with stagnation or vulnerability with weakness.
I rise softer now, but stronger.
I lead slower, but with more purpose.
I love deeper, but with clearer boundaries.
That, to me, is real strength — the kind that glows quietly from the inside out.

Teaching My Children the Rhythm of Growth

One evening, my daughter came home discouraged after making a mistake at school. She said,
"Mom, I feel like I keep messing up."
I smiled, remembering all the times I had said the same to myself. So I told her,
"You're not messing up. You're learning how to rise better next time."
That's what I want all my children — and every woman reading this — to understand:
You will fall. You will falter. You will face seasons that feel uncertain. But none of it means you're failing. It means you're becoming.

The Science of Grace

In neuroscience, we know that every time we choose self-compassion instead of self-criticism, we actually rewire the brain's default pathways. Grace is not just spiritual — it's biological.
When you give yourself permission to be human, you calm the amygdala, engage the prefrontal cortex, and create emotional safety.
In that safety, growth thrives.
You think more clearly, recover more quickly, and act more intentionally.
Grace, then, is the soil in which your next rise takes root.

Reflection Prompts:
As you come to the close of this journey, take a moment to reflect deeply:
1. What parts of yourself have you rediscovered through this process?
2. What are you ready to release — expectations, guilt, comparison, perfectionism?
3. How will you nurture your glow in this next season?
4. What does "rising differently" look like for you now?

Glow Practice: The Mirror of Becoming
Stand in front of the mirror, not to critique yourself, but to meet your reflection as if she were an old friend.
Look into your eyes and say:
"Thank you for surviving."
"Thank you for growing."
"Thank you for rising — again and again."

Take a slow breath. Smile gently.
You are not the woman you once were — and that's the beauty of it.
Because this isn't the end of your story.
It's the continuation of a lifelong rhythm:
Reflect. Recalibrate. Rise.
Each time softer. Each time wiser. Each time brighter.
And that — that's how you lead with glow.

Author's Note

Thank you for allowing me to walk beside you on this journey. May your glow continue to shine brighter with each new season of your life.

— With love and light,
Kimly Hoang-Nakata, M.Ed
Award -Winning Educator & Author | MindSmart Learning Specialist , CEO, Founder at Achieve Education, MindSmart Learning & Glow Circle

About the Author

Kimly Hoang-Nakata, M.Ed. is an award-winning educator, author, MindSmart Learning Specialist, CEO and Founder at Achieve Education, MindSmart Learning & Glow Circle. Known for her signature message —"Lead with light, not with pressure" Kimly blends neuroscience, psychology, and storytelling to help students, women, and families rediscover their calm, confidence, and purpose —and rise with unshakable clarity.

For years, she dedicated her career to shaping young minds, but along the way discovered a deeper truth: true success doesn't begin in the classroom —it begins within. Blending wisdom and heart, Kimly brings science to life through stories that empower others to learn, grow, and thrive. Kimly is passionate about inspiring purpose-driven growth and resilience. Her work has been featured in *Global Thought Leaders TV & Magazine*. She also contributed to *The Impact Leaders* alongside Shark Tank's Kevin Harrington and other award-winning authors recognized by the International Impact Book Awards.

A mother of three and Author of the Year Finalist, Kimly has inspired audiences across schools, organizations, and women's leadership circles to transform burnout into brilliance and purpose into presence. Through *The Glow Community*, she teaches that when a woman glows from within, she doesn't just change her life —she changes the atmosphere around her.

To learn more about *Emotional Leadership in Parenthood*, mastermind workshops, MindSmart Learning or to join her *Glow Circle* for inspiration and support in womanhood, please email: Support@achieve.education or visit: https://www.achieve.education

References

Amabile, T. M., & Kramer, S. J. (2011). *The progress principle: Using small wins to ignite joy, engagement, and creativity at work.* Harvard Business Review Press.

Barsade, S. G. (2002). The ripple effect: Emotional contagion and its influence on group behavior. *Administrative Science Quarterly, 47*(4), 644–675.

Beckes, L., & Coan, J. A. (2011). Social baseline theory: The role of social proximity in emotion and economy of action. *Social and Personality Psychology Compass, 5*(12), 976–988.

Coan, J. A., Schaefer, H. S., & Davidson, R. J. (2006). Lending a hand: Social regulation of the neural response to threat. *Psychological Science, 17*(12), 1032–1039.

Hatfield, E., Cacioppo, J. T., & Rapson, R. L. (1994). *Emotional contagion.* Cambridge University Press.

Keysers, C., & Gazzola, V. (2010). Social neuroscience: Mirror neurons recorded in humans. *Annual Review of Neuroscience, 33*, 337–359.

Laborde, S., Allen, M. S., Borges, U., Mosley, E., & Gendolla, G. H. E. (2022). Heart rate variability and self-regulation: A roundtable. *Applied Psychophysiology and Biofeedback, 47*(1), 1–19.

Lieberman, M. D., Eisenberger, N. I., Crockett, M. J., Tom, S. M., Pfeifer, J. H., & Way, B. M. (2007). Putting feelings into words: Affect labeling disrupts amygdala activity to affective stimuli. *Psychological Science, 18*(5), 421–428.

Monsell, S. (2003). Task switching. *Trends in Cognitive Sciences, 7*(3), 134–140.

Mullainathan, S., & Shafir, E. (2013). *Scarcity: Why having too little means so much.* Times Books.

Neff, K. D. (2003). Self-compassion: An alternative conceptualization of a healthy attitude toward oneself. *Self and Identity, 2*(2), 85–101.

Neff, K. D., & Germer, C. K. (2013). A pilot study and randomized controlled trial of the Mindful Self-Compassion program. *Journal of Clinical Psychology, 69*(1), 28–44.

Rizzolatti, G., & Craighero, L. (2004). The mirror-neuron system. *Annual Review of Neuroscience, 27*, 169–192.

Russo, M. A., Santarelli, D. M., & O'Rourke, D. (2017). The physiological effects of slow breathing in the healthy human. *Breathe, 13*(4), 298–309.

van der Kolk, B. (2014). *The body keeps the score: Brain, mind, and body in the healing of trauma.* Viking.

Wetherell, M. A., Smith, M. A., Aitchison, T. C., et al. (2017). A systematic review of the cortisol response to academic stress. *Stress, 20*(1), 1–14.